ROCKFORD PUBLIC LIBRARY

Rockford, Illinois

www.rockfordpubliclibrary.org

815-965-9511

KWANZAA

A TRUE BOOK

by

Dana Meachen Rau

Children's Press®

A Division of Grolier Publishing

New York London Hong Kong Sydney
Danbury, Connecticut

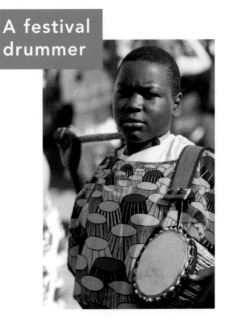

A festival
drummer

Reading Consultant
Linda Cornwell
*Coordinator of School Quality
and Professional Improvement
Indiana State Teachers
Association*

Author's Dedication
*For my friends at the
Farmington Library*

Library of Congress Cataloging-in-Publication Data

Rau, Dana Meachen, 1971-
    Kwanzaa / by Dana Meachen Rau.
        p.   cm. — (A true book)
    Includes index.
    Summary: Discusses the origins, symbols, and celebration of Kwanzaa, the
holiday that focuses on African American history, culture, and experiences.
    ISBN 0-516-21517-5
    1. Kwanzaa—Juvenile literature. 2. Afro-Americans—Social life and
customs—Juvenile literature. 3. United States—Social life and customs—
Juvenile literature. [1. Kwanzaa. 2. Holidays. 3. Afro-Americans—Social
life and customs.] I. Title. II. Series.

GT4403 .R38 2000
394.261—dc21   99-086741

Contents

Kwanzaa is a family celebration.

A Special Holiday

The month of December is filled with celebrations. Christmas and Chanukah are two holidays that are popular at this time of year. There is also a special holiday celebrated by many African-Americans. It is called Kwanzaa.

Kwanzaa is a time when African-American families gather

This grandmother reads a Kwanzaa story to her grandchildren.

to remember their history and look forward to their future. Children listen to stories about their African ancestors, sing African songs, and feast on African foods. The holiday is filled with ceremonies, music, friends, and gift giving.

6

How Kwanzaa Began

Many holidays have been celebrated for hundreds of years. Kwanzaa, however, has only been a part of family traditions since the 1960s. The ideas behind Kwanzaa began in Africa.

Long ago, Africa was filled with great kingdoms, art, music, and traditions. One of these

African ancestors tilled the soil (above) and later celebrated the harvest with drums and singing (right).

traditions was harvest festivals. Villagers all over Africa farmed the land. At the end of a good season, people celebrated to give thanks for their crops.

Europeans came to Africa and captured many black Africans. They sold the Africans

Africans were forced from their homeland and sold as property.

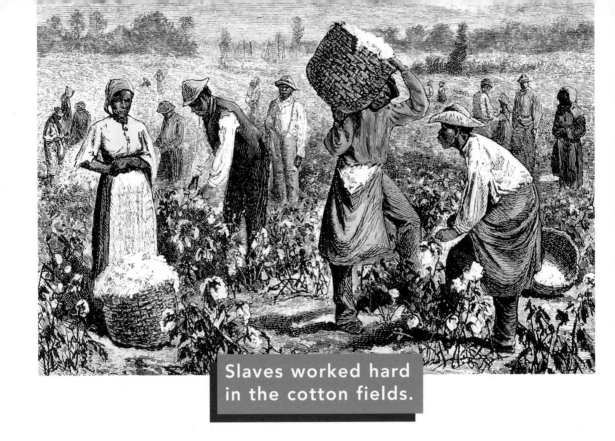

Slaves worked hard in the cotton fields.

as slaves. In the United States, the slaves were forced to work on slave owners' farms. The slaves were treated like property instead of people. The slaves lost many of their African traditions.

Not everyone in the United States agreed with slavery. It was popular in the South, where there were many farms. But many people in the North were against slavery. So the

Once slaves, these men fought as U.S. soldiers during the Civil War.

North and the South fought the American Civil War (1861–65). The North won, and soon slavery was against the law.

But black Americans still were not treated as well as white Americans. In the 1960s, many blacks were finally able to gain the same rights as white people. During this time, a man named Dr. Maulana Karenga was an African-American leader. He thought a holiday would be a good way to help

Today, African-Americans honor leaders of the past, such as Dr. Martin Luther King, who helped them share the same rights as white people.

At a Kwanzaa concert,
candles add warmth and joy.

African-Americans create strong families, learn about their history, and unite as a group of people.

Dr. Karenga created a new holiday that was like the African harvest festivals of long ago. In 1966, he created Kwanzaa. The word *kwanzaa* comes from the Swahili phrase *matunda ya kwanza* which means "first fruits" of the harvest. (Swahili is an African language.)

The Meaning of Kwanzaa

Kwanzaa lasts seven days, from December 26 to January 1. Several million people celebrate Kwanzaa in the United States, Canada, England, the Caribbean, Africa, and other countries around the world.

Kwanzaa is based on seven principles, or important ideas.

They are called the *Nguzo Saba* (En-GOO-zoh Sah-BAH). Each of the seven days of Kwanzaa is centered around a different principle. The principles are: unity, self-determination, collective work and responsibility, cooperative economics, purpose, creativity, and faith.

Unity means the coming together of the family, the community, and all African-Americans.

Self-determination means that one will stand up for oneself and decide one's own future.

Volunteers help serve food at a soup kitchen.

Collective work and responsibility means to work with others and help solve problems together.

Cooperative economics means to support businesses run by African-Americans.

Purpose means remembering the traditions of past African relatives.

A beautiful mural gives the neighborhood a sense of pride.

Creativity means making the community beautiful.

Faith means believing in family, leaders, and other African-Americans. It also means having faith in oneself and dreams for the future.

The Seven Principles

These are the Swahili words for the Seven Principles, or Nguzo Saba:

umoja (oo-MOE-jah): **unity**

kujichagulia (koo-jee-cha-goo-LEE-ah): **self-determination**

ujima (oo-JEE-mah): **collective work and responsibility**

ujamaa (oo-JAH-mah): **cooperative economics**

nia (nee-AH): **purpose**

kuumba (koo-OOM-bah): **creativity**

imani (ee-MAH-nee): **faith**

Each candle stands for one of the principles celebrated during Kwanzaa.

Symbols of Kwanzaa

When a family sets the Kwanzaa table, it includes seven important items.

First, the family lays down a straw placemat. This mat symbolizes African tradition. Next, a candleholder, called a *kinara*, is placed on the mat. It holds seven candles. Each

The kinara is fully lit on the last night of Kwanzaa.

candle stands for one of the seven principles. There is one black candle in the center, three red candles on the left, and three green candles on the right. Red, green, and black are also the colors of the African-American flag.

The family places fruit on the table to remind them of the African harvest festivals of long ago. An ear of corn for each child in the house is also put on the table. The

family takes out a cup called the unity cup. It will be used during a special ceremony. Finally, the table may also hold gifts for the children. The gifts are meant to encourage the seven principles.

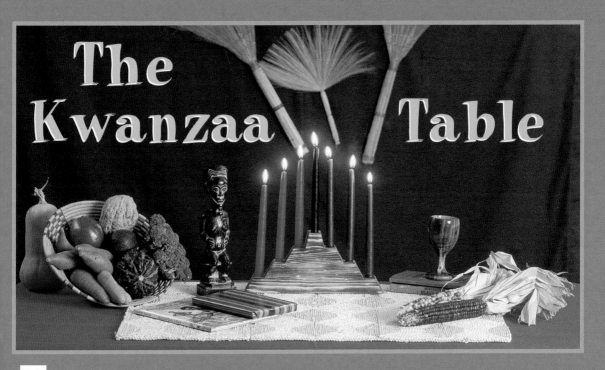

The Kwanzaa Table

The seven symbols on a Kwanzaa table include:

Mkeka (M-KAY-cah): **a straw placemat**

Kinara (Kee-NAH-rah): **a holder for seven candles**

Mishumaa (Mee-SHOO-maah): **the candles**

Mazao (Ma-ZOW): **fruit**

Muhindi (Moo-HEEN-dee): **an ear of corn for each child in the home**

Kikombe cha umoja (Kee-COAM-bay chah-oo-MOE-jah): **a unity cup**

Zawadi (Sah-WAH-dee): **gifts**

How Families Celebrate

Each day of Kwanzaa may start with a question. One person asks *"Habari gani?"* which means, "What is the news?" The other person answers with the principle of the day.

Usually before dinner, a leader calls the family together

Each family member takes part in the nightly celebration.

around the Kwanzaa table. The children then light the candles on the kinara. First they light the black center candle. Then, the other candles are lit. On the first day of Kwanzaa, the center candle is lit, and then one of the red candles on the left. The next night, the center candle is lit, the one on the left, and then one of the green candles on the right. This continues back and forth over all the nights until all of the candles are lit on the last day of Kwanzaa.

After the children light the candle of the day's principle, each person takes a turn talking about the importance of the principle. They may talk about what the principle means to them. They may tell a traditional folktale or a story of a famous African-American. They may even sing an African song.

Stories about great African-Americans of the past are read.

An important part of Kwanzaa is remembering ancestors. To honor great people of the past, the leader uses the unity cup to pour juice or water into a bowl. Then he drinks from the cup and says *"Harambee!"* Everyone repeats "Harambee!" seven times and

Drinking the unity cup together gives special meaning to the ceremony.

drinks from the cup. "Haram-bee" means "Let's all pull together." Family members call out names. Everyone thinks about the important values taught by these people.

Next, gifts may be given. Sometimes gifts are saved for the last night of Kwanzaa. The gifts are not simply toys or games. They have special meaning and refer to the principle of the day. Many times, the gifts are homemade,

These children admire an African item made long ago (above). Someone might receive an *ankh (right)*, a symbol of life, as a Kwanzaa gift.

educational, or cultural. After the ceremony is finished, the family sits down to a meal together.

The Kwanzaa Song

Families may sing the Kwanzaa song as part of their celebration.

**Kwanzaa is a holiday
Kwanzaa, Kwanzaa,
  Kwanzaa
Is an African holiday
Seven principles
Seven candles
Seven black days for
  the African
Kwanzaa Yenu Iwe Na Heri
(Happy Kwanzaa!)**

Many voices make the Kwanzaa song sound even happier.

The Final Feast

The week of family celebrations leads up to the biggest party of Kwanzaa—the *Karamu*. It is a large feast held on the night before the last day of Kwanzaa, December 31. Family and friends gather for an evening of good food, dancing and

Dancing at a public
Kwanzaa celebration

music, storytelling and speech-
es. It is an important time to
pass on African traditions and
celebrate African culture.

Food is an important part of the celebration. People eat African dishes, often from all parts of Africa. Everyone takes part in preparing the

This feast includes a baked ham (center) marked with a "K" for Kwanzaa.

meal. The food might include millet, spiced pepper balls, or benne cakes. "Benne" means sesame seeds. They are eaten for good luck.

The next day, the last day of Kwanzaa, the principle of faith is discussed. This includes faith in the African-American community as a whole, as well as faith in oneself and one's dreams for the future. Children are always reminded that even though it is January 1, the spirit of Kwanzaa does not end. The principles celebrated during Kwanzaa are not just for the holiday. They are to be a part of life every day of the year.

A children's choir prepares
for a church concert.

To Find Out More

Here are some additional resources to help you learn more about Kwanzaa and other holidays:

 **Books**

Corwin, Judith Hoffman. **Kwanzaa Crafts.** Franklin Watts, 1995.

Hoyt-Goldsmith, Diane. **Celebrating Kwanzaa.** Holiday House, 1993.

Johnson, Dolores. **The Children's Book of Kwanzaa: A Guide to Celebrating the Holiday.** Atheneum, 1996.

Washington, Donna L. **The Story of Kwanzaa.** HarperCollins, 1996.

Organizations and Online Sites

Anacostia Museum and Center for African American History and Culture
1901 Fort Place, SE
Washington, DC 20020
http://www.si.edu/anacostia

This Smithsonian Institution museum is devoted to increasing knowledge about African-American history and culture through its programs and exhibits.

Festivals.com
RSL Interactive
1001 Alaskan Way
Pier 55, Suite 288
Seattle, WA 98101
http://www.festivals.com/

Visit this site to find out about all types of festivals, holidays, and fairs around the world.

Kwanzaa Information Center
http://melanet.com/ kwanzaa/

This site tells of the history of Kwanzaa and how to celebrate it in your home.

Important Words

ancestor a member of your family who lived a long time ago

ceremony a formal act performed in honor of an event or special occasion

crop a plant grown in large amounts, usually for food

harvest festival a celebration to give thanks for a good crop

principle a basic truth, law, or belief

right something that the law says you can have or do, as in the right to vote

symbol an object that stands for something else

tradition a custom, idea, or belief that is handed down from one generation to the next

Index

Meet the Author

Ever since Dana Meachen Rau can remember, she has loved to write. A graduate of Trinity College in Hartford, Connecticut, Dana works as a children's book editor and has authored many books for children, including biographies, nonfiction, early readers, and historical fiction. She has also won awards for her short stories.

When Dana is not writing, she is doing her favorite things—watching movies, eating chocolate, and drawing pictures—with her husband Chris and son Charlie in Farmington, Connecticut.